HANDLE WITH CARE

7 Essentials to Prepare, Pack and Propel For a Career Transition

Pamela Burkett-Jones

Publishing Service By: Pen Legacy®
Cover By: Pixel Studios (Bosnia and Herzegovina)
Editing Services By: Candice "Ordered Steps" Johnson
Formatting By: Carla Dean, U Can Mark My Word

Library of Congress Cataloging – in- Publication Data has been applied for.

Paperback ISBN: 9781736411254

PRINTED IN THE UNITED STATES OF AMERICA.

Dedication

This book is dedicated to my late father, Roosevelt, "Teddy" for your relentless example of being unstoppable and never allowing unfortunate circumstances to get in the way of personal goals, overall happiness, and your number one priority to provide for your family. Your actions truly inspired and motivated me to always keep going and never give up on my goals, desires, and dreams.

Table of Contents

HANDLE WITH CARE

7 Essentials to Prepare, Pack and Propel For a Career Transition

INTRODUCTION

Congratulations! I am super excited you have decided to embark on a career change. This may have been prompted by a desire to find a career which is more fulfilling and rewarding; if this is the case, you've chosen the right book!

A career move is no different than moving from one residence to another, as both require careful planning to prepare for what lies ahead. Several factors must be considered prior to such life-altering adjustments: price, location, accessibility, and happiness, but you must be committed to the process. Transitioning is not always as difficult as it sounds, but it requires patience and planning to avoid stress and confusion. Everything we ever need to transition successfully can be found within or accessible. But as the saying goes, "If it was easy, everyone would be doing it."

In December 2017, I said goodbye to my employer of 27 years. Was I worried? Absolutely. You see, my exit came from the desire to *fire* my employer in order to find happiness. I had 32 years in my profession under my belt, and I knew it was time to embark on a journey befitting of my mindset, needs, and most importantly, my dreams. I have more life behind me than I do ahead of me, so I had to make every moment count.

As I cleaned my office, I inventoried the many things I collected over the years, as well as the woman I had become. The lessons and accomplishments were essential to my career. Even though I had vacated other positions in the agency, this time was different. I was packing for a pivotal shift. My career was getting a makeover, and if I did not pack with care, I may have discarded or left essential things behind. As I walked out the door with my box in hand, I was ready to explore what life had for me.

After achieving great strides during my transition, I followed my new passion of coaching individuals through their own career transitions. My passion has led me to become the founder and executive director of my own coaching and consulting company—*Proactive*

Coaching and Consulting. I am a certified coach, speaker, trainer, and college adjunct professor, teaching criminal justice. Now this may seem like overload, but I am at peace doing what satisfies me. I love connecting with so many wonderful dreamers who are working on becoming the best version of themselves with me as their coach.

There is life after your profession.

Life is meant to try new things; there are many options out there for us to try, fail, and overcome. The rewards of a well-lived life are seizing opportunities while you have time. That may look like travel for some, or job-hopping until finding the best role for others. This book will help you prepare and pack to propel you to your next career move, regardless if it's with an employer, starting your own business or simply volunteering with your favorite organization.

My goal to teach and coach you through the seven essential steps of my *Moving Box Methodology*. This methodology propelled me from employee, to freedom, to happiness. Isn't that the goal? Doesn't a happy life sound amazing? Let me tell you it is, and if I knew before what I know now, I would have packed earlier.

My process removes the burden from transition, and births a sense of freedom as you prepare your *Moving Box*. Throughout these pages, we will dive deep into your box's significance, its contents, and you as the packer. You will also have the opportunity to take a moment to reflect on adjusting or aligning your documents with guaranteed execution in the thoughts sections.

If you're ready to take this leap of faith, I'm ready to help you prepare, pack and propel towards your next career path.

Are you ready? Let's go.

MOVING BOX METHODOLOGY

Any move begins with gathering the most important element in structuring, organizing and protecting valuable possessions: ***the moving box***. Even though it is simply cardboard, this box is the most crucial part of the process. Boxes are effective when transporting our things from one location to the next; however, there is a bigger significance the box has than we think. Allow me to introduce you to my method and how this box plays a significant role in your transition.

When I was transitioning careers, my perception of the moving box changed. I realized my belongings gave the box purpose. That's when I combined the concept of career transitioning with the box's significance—the ***Moving Box Methodology***. Who would have believed a brown box would be instrumental in helping you properly prepare, pack and propel into the most important step of your life? Since this concept is new, I have adapted a core strategy within my business which allows me to share how this methodology came to fruition, and how it benefits you.

After spending nearly three decades employed by one agency, packing was quite the experience when it came time to transition. The years' worth of memorabilia, trinkets, and documents were no easy task to box up, to say the least.

Before I began packing, I strategized what was necessary to take with me. I took inventory and constructed a list of what aligned with where I was heading. As my box took form, I examined what was significant for my next chapter. It was also important for me to consider the tangible and intangible things when packing.

- Tangible: Things you can physically touch such as office furniture, supplies, plaques or awards, etc.
- Intangible: Things which don't physically exist and can't be touched, such as qualities and characteristics.

As I became clear on what I was moving, I packed my valuables. Once carefully packed, I constructed a list identifying the things inside, aligning with where I was heading.

My next step added protection to keep my valuables safe from being broken, shifting, or worst-case scenario, extreme damage. I took extra precautions to secure everything with foam paper or bubble wrap and placed them gingerly inside. For an added layer of protection, I sealed the box to keep the contents from becoming compromised.

"Pamela, is all of this necessary?" you may ask. My answer? YES. Protecting every aspect of our lives is essential in preparing for the next stage.

Now that the contents are secured, it's time to address the outside of the box.

Have you ever paid attention to what's printed on moving box? The phrase **THIS SIDE UP** is prominently displayed, along with graphics of arrows pointing upward. As trivial as this may seem, the graphics provide clear directions, giving carriers handling instructions to prevent spilling or disrupting the contents.

FRAGILE, **HANDLE WITH CARE**, **DO NOT STACK**, and **CAUTION, HEAVY** are also printed on the boxes; however, my favorite is: **CAUTION HEAVY**

TEAM LIFT. In addition to words, symbols such as an umbrella (*keep dry or keep in a cool, dry place*), a drinking glass (*fragile items inside*), or two hands holding up a box (*handle with care*) appear on the outside. You may not have realized a simple cardboard box needed so many elements, but the labels, symbols and words are there to protect the contents. Without them, there is no guidance on how to handle them properly.

Imagine what can happen to your belongings if there is no indication of what's inside. There is a strong chance the mover may mishandle the boxes during transport. I have witnessed boxes tossed around damaging the contents or placed in compromising places destroying the contents stored inside. Just think of all the times you have shipped packages or used a moving company, only to find a complete mess upon delivery.

Now that my box was properly packed, it was time for me to propel. I can honestly say I was well-equipped and ready for my new destination. I completed my research, seeking knowledge from reliable sources. Being prepared and informed for the road ahead is essential in making the transition smooth. The more you know, the less you have to assume, stress, and worry about.

As I vacated my office, the boxes caught the attention of others who worked in the office building. Some of them bombarded me with questions.

"Do you need help?"

"Where are you going?"

"What is all of that stuff?"

I can still see the smiles as I answered their questions one by one. Knowing the significance of everything inside the boxes made it easy to explain; I could attest to the story behind each chip, scratch, dent, perfection or imperfection. My answers were filled with grace because I had peace. I was full of confidence, knowing I carefully loaded my box with meaningful things. I'll never forget my response when someone asked me, "What are you carrying everything, including the kitchen sink?" "I have a box full of essential items needed for my next move," I responded with pride.

You see, I refused to carry junk in my moving boxes. As a matter of fact, I had no issues throwing things out, shredding, or giving things away. I felt it was my duty to pass along information or give things to others which would help make them comfortable or their jobs easier.

As I hauled the boxes to my car, officers on guard as security at the front desk asked if I needed help. It would have been insane for me to turn them down, since it was not a one-person job. When they saw how heavy the boxes were, they asked what was inside. When reaching this essential phase of transition, be prepared and don't hesitate to explain what's in your box. I will always appreciate those who helped me move to my next destination.

Now with my *Moving Box Methodology* along with careful planning and preparation, I was hired on my first new career interview during the transitioning period. I was granted a new professional life after retirement from the criminal justice field, and it did not stop there. While going through the company's mandatory hiring process, I was able to reflect on my journey and examine what I had collected through the years.

Even though I was moving forward, the second phase of my transition caused me to rethink things once again. You know when you feel there is *more*? My warm feelings told me I had accomplished something great, and there was more to my story.

From my reflections surrounding the *Moving Box Methodology,* are you ready to implement this concept into your transition? The elements of my box coupled with my preparedness for my next was crucial for me. As you read further, it is important to remember your moving box reflects you and what you have to offer. Throughout the next chapters, you'll learn what I call the *7 Essentials,* and how they helped me successfully transition. The *7 Essentials* we will uncover are:

- **Pack with caution.** The necessary mindset when packing your box.

- **Understand what you are holding.** Know the significance of each item you have.
- **Add security measures**. Understand the importance of sealing and padding the box.
- **Pay attention to labels**. Be aware how you look on paper, i.e. - resumes, cover letters, and applications.
- **Check out the forwarding address**. Thoroughly research new or potential destinations.
- **Ask for help**. Embrace the importance of networking and the role people play in your transition.
- **Be prepared to provide detailed explanation**. Preparing for the interview and celebrating the new journey ahead.

By following the essentials, you'll be well on your way towards a seamless career change. This is everything you need to equip yourself for a successful transition.

It's time to gather those boxes and execute the *Moving Box Methodology*.

PACK WITH CAUTION

As you prepare for your transition, consider the needs, feelings, and emotions you have for such a permanent change. Although we experience various types of moves, this book only focuses on your *professional* moves. For many, changing professions stirs up uncertainty and fear, regardless if you have accepted another position within your company, at another agency, as an entrepreneur, or embarking on a brand-new career path.

Our emotions determine if an offer is the right for us and bring clarity to address our feelings accordingly. Ignoring our intuition clouds our response and what we really want, ultimately hindering us from propelling forward. As strong and well put together we think we are, this is not the time to ignore your gut instinct, because they will find a way to prove they were right in other areas of your journey. We often hear people say the space between what we want and what we receive is our mindset. Our perception greatly influences how hard we will work and what we will settle for in comfort.

I understand the journey to better is scary, but I want you to ask yourself what is it costing you to stay where you are. What can pursuing your goals afford you? What about a promotion? What can betting on YOU guarantee? Be careful not to become stagnate in your comfort zone. Productive moves are difficult to achieve without convincing yourself the change will be overall beneficial.

Speaking from experience, let me assure you are more ready to transition than you think. Be open to the short and long term benefits this change will spark in your life. Before we move forward, take a moment to review some things you will need to get fully prepared.

MINDSET SHIFTING

Reaching our goals requires shifting our thinking. Start by believing it can be done. Dwelling on what we lack in our current situation and surroundings keeps us from preparing properly to transition into greater. Instead, we treat it as changing locations with a slight adjustment.

I'm sure your decision to make the transition was not to yield the same results from your previous career. You are not searching for a temporary move, in case things do not work out – you want a new career, a new foundation, never to look back again, correct?

FEELINGS

The journey to new means releasing the old. The goal is not to go through all the trouble of transitioning, only to revert back to what we left behind, or worse - switch to something else in the future. Most of us make a change because we are ready for something new, more fulfilling, exciting and pertinent to our goals. It's normal to want to reach new heights taking us to places we never imagined reaching in our lifetime.

EMOTIONS

Emotions are where we seek the answer to our "why." If we do not carefully think through our move, we may find ourselves repeating the same patterns in our next career.

Start by creating a bigger vision than your last destination, and align your emotions with it. Consider this: When preparing to move into a house which is under construction, the homeowner meets with the builder or his or her representative to select color patterns, carpet and wood finishes, cabinets and so on. They imagine living in the house before it is even built – mentally and physically preparing for what's to come. For many, a new home has been a goal for some time. However, they were not ready to make it happen until the perfect time with careful planning. In most cases, the house is completely different from their current or old home. The move is bigger than their current circumstances.

Please be aware this is the time negative emotions may show up. Worry, fear, doubt, confusion, and sadness cause stress and overtakes us if not managed. Even though these are common emotions during transition, don't let your feelings make you second-guess yourself. I have witnessed so many people make premature decisions without investigating the cause behind the emotion.

During various stages of my transition, I was frequently overwhelmed with sadness. Don't get me wrong - I was not sad because I was moving on; however, after spending several decades of my life growing within a single agency, I was saying goodbye. Goodbye to personal and professional connections. Farewell to the experiences – both good and bad, I was leaving behind as I embarked on my fresh start. Eventually, doubt clouded my decision.

What if the new boss or coworkers are not easy to get along with?

What if they are not willing to teach or train me the ins and outs of the position?

What if…

Fear kicked in, but I swiftly reversed negativity by admitting that even though I was going to miss being in a familiar environment, I've never had a problem meeting new people or learning new things. How did I trudge forward? Simple: By realizing my fears were unfounded. I was confident in what I brought to the table, and if they did not think I could handle the position, I would not have been hired.

I knew I was the best candidate for the job, and a great asset to move their mission forward. I reassured myself I could seamlessly cultivate personal relationships in my next chapter. Moving on didn't mean losing personal friendships. My colleagues were a phone call or drive away, genuine relationships would be able to withstand separation.

POSITIVE SELF-TALK

Before packing, your mind and emotions must be in alignment to avoid talking yourself out of what you have worked, prayed and prepared for in your next chapter. I will also advise you to watch your language, what you speak to yourself and say to others. See, manifestation comes through our words and conversations, powerful both internally and externally.

Further into your transition, self-doubt, fear, and uncertainty will invade your thoughts at the first sign of confusion, dysfunction, and mishaps. It is imperative to stand firm on your decision, eliminating room for distractions or quitting. Your language from here on should reflect strength and commitment.

In addition to identifying self-sabotaging behavior, watch out for naysayers who will have you second guessing yourself. I'm not sure about you, but I am easily annoyed when people project their fears, inability to achieve their goals or manifest their desires by belittling your dreams. Instead of supporting, they fire criticism in your plans.

If someone is committed to devouring your goals with their limited beliefs, you don't need them. You may consider them in high regard, maybe even a "bestie." But if they cannot see your greatness for themselves, they would not understand or show a positive attitude towards your move. They are not the wise counsel you need. Watch and identify those who are in your corner and would not distract you from your goals.

I often advise clients to consult with successful practitioners in their desired field. Find individuals to speak with who have successfully accomplished what they were aiming for to share best practices. This action simplifies the process and relieves individuals from the fear of the unknown. Remember - the people you surround yourself with while preparing to move should be those who can help prepare you for the journey.

"Your Why" Coaching Exercises:

To clarify your why, complete this quick exercise: Make two lists. The first reflects the reasons you have decided to transition; the second reflects the positive results which can come from it.

Propelling Exercises:

Based on the packing elements, what mindset shifts, emotions, feelings or self-talk are preventing you from moving forward? Negative emotions are distractions designed to deter us from focusing on our next destination. Below, jot down the emotions to help take the first step of your transition.

____

____

____

____

____

____

____

____

____

____

____

____

____

____

How are you feeling? Are things becoming a bit clearer? As you continue reading, it is my hope you become more in tune with the perception transition brings. Self-help author and motivational speaker Wayne Dyer once said, *"If you change the way you look at things, the way you look at things will change."*

This quote resonates with me because when you think about it, the objects we sometimes consider big, no longer seem like it in the end. This helps us appreciate where we have been, and look forward to where we are going. Embracing this quote is also beneficial before, during and after our transition because it challenges us to reshape how we view ourselves, others and the world. When our perspective changes, we become laser focused and unstoppable. Things which were once invisible becomes visible; obstacles become smaller, eventually disappearing.

For example, I often refer to *looking through the rearview mirror while driving.*

Have you ever taken a road trip and noticed signs indicating the distance between where you are to the nearest city with nothing other than the road, trees and rest stops in sight? Once you get closer the city, huge skyscrapers, sports stadiums and historic landmarks come into view. Passing through the city limits, you ever notice how things appear smaller and smaller? At one point, you check the rear-view mirror - what was once large in your eyes dwindles into tiny specs. Even though the objects fade away, you are still on the road towards your next destination.

In the above scenario, the city became a distraction, drawing your attention away from the road, but you drove by and stayed the course. If you come across a distraction, challenge or stumbling block, identify it and find solutions to stay focused on what's ahead. At this point, you should be confident, know what you want, what resources are available, how to get there, and be able to pivot without returning to where you came from as you strive for your new destination.

DECLUTTER TO MOVE FORWARD

Now that we have our focus, clarity and spirit in check, it is time to start assembling our box. But before we pack, here is another tip to only take the things we need on our move:

It's time to declutter.

Decluttering, purging, and discarding things that will not serve you on your next stop makes the boxes lighter. I saw this part of my phase as my opportunity to help make others' jobs easier. Consideration and kindness goes a long way; we never know the learning curve the next employee may encounter while transitioning into their new role, just like you. Small acts of kindness are gifts which keeps on giving. Be the light, so someone can be a light for you.

As you declutter, evaluate what you have collected, and how it aligns with your transition. This is where you question your own values as they relate to who you presently are, and who you need to become.

When I became a certified coach, I learned there are two types of values: fear-based and conscious-based.

- Fear values come into effect when we are avoiding an undesired outcome or negative consequences.
- Conscious values allow us to make positive decisions aimed towards passions and goals.

Which value are you operating in?

As you pack, keep this question in mind to answer the below questions:

- Why is this important to me?
- How does it reflect who I am?
- How does it contribute to my future?
- What does it say about me?

Once you have answered these questions, you are ready to begin packing the personal and professional representations of you. Self-awareness is vital when considering what is packed, as it identifies who you are, where you have been and your potential.

Whatever is in your box should have significant meaning and protected as such. If you have been in a position for an extended time, it is not uncommon to forget what you actually possess; it is perfectly fine to take your time packing everything you need. It is also helpful to consult with others who may have been with you throughout your career to help recall accomplishments and achievements you may have overlooked. Remember, how and what you pack tells where you have been and the accomplishments you have achieved.

As you gather your belongings, it is not wrong to discard things which hinders our ability to believe in ourselves generating feelings of self-doubt. It is also not wrong to discard items which does not help us. Focusing on the wrong things could lead to producing internal blocks and potentially get in the way of a successful transition. Internal blocks are limited beliefs in our abilities, preconceived assumptions, wrong interpretations and made-up barriers. For example, maybe a project did not turn out as planned or was not executed due to distractions, outside limitations or evaluations which were not an accurate representation of our hard work or determination.

During this time, focus on which items accurately depict your achievements and the mark you have left on the company's reputation. Reflect on your strengths and ability to succeed in the future. The contents you have developed are unique to you, which makes you stand out.

Preparation is necessary when accepting new assignments or positions. Every time I moved on - even before retiring, I only carried what was necessary to my new position. Trust me, before I embodied this methodology, I packed so much that was not beneficial to my new role. However, I knew in the long run there would be some value in it.

Following retirement, I was offered the opportunity to work in a field where I thought I would not be considered because of my age; however, after the hiring manager viewed my digital footprint, I was offered the position. The same way I have managed to stay employed and gain new employment, you can too. My steps are detailed in the *Moving Box Methodology*. Proceed with caution as you gather your belongings, and consider what is useful in the long haul. See you in the next chapter.

WHAT ARE YOU HOLDING?

As we go through life, we pick things up along the way. There are skills we have to build, become acclimated to, and eventually make our own. In this chapter, we'll reflect on the abilities and opportunities which put us in places we never imagined.

As time progresses, we become accustomed to our daily activities which causes us to overlook the opportunities within our reach which could propel us. Are you guilty of seeing the win without 100% understanding its value? Often, we store things away, promising to get back to it…only to forget its relevance in our lives and future.

Out of sight, out of mind, is how we fail to execute or return to the opportunities we place on hold. How many times have you begun clearing out and uncovering things you thought you had lost or forgotten about, only to realize its value when you consider giving it to someone else? On the flip side, it could be something you decide to bring along. In this chapter, we will see if what you have packed is necessary.

If we are not careful, we end up with multiple boxes jammed with unnecessary items, overlooking what is really important to our transition. Once we understand what we need to keep, the reward is seeing just how far we have come, which keeps us on the right track. Sure there are distractions: souvenirs, tokens and memorabilia to remind us of the past, while making us stronger, better and wiser. The majority of our experiences shape us into the person we are. With all that being said, allow me to ask, "What are you holding?"

This stage of the *Moving Box Methodology* focused on filling our box with achievements, reminders of accomplishments, awards souvenirs, memorabilia which includes intangible items we store away. Noteworthy items are not necessarily receiving recognition at an awards banquet or gala nor does being rewarded by a superior for your hard work. Recognizing your hard work can also be an intangible prize; non-tangible wins come in handy as proof of your experience and magnifies your skills.

Once your boxes are packed, create a manifesto of what is inside to alert packers for future reference. Deliveries arrive with an itemized list of contents; we should do the same. Our internal "packing lists" are crucial in recognizing our talents and abilities. They bring awareness of what we bring to the table for potential employers, clients and business partners, and showcase our credentials.

Your transition may not arrive on the heels of a long journey like mine; yours can be much shorter. However, transitioning careers can happen at any time in your life, whether it is six months or forty years. It is up to you to make the decision when.

The collection period for my box was extremely long, as I had thirty-two years' worth of things to sift through - five years in one agency and twenty-seven in another in the same field. The key to my transition was starting the process five years before transitioning.

I had plenty of work in order to clean, purge, and declutter. Granting myself permission to understand the significance of the tangible and intangible items within my reach and possession, I noticed the impact I had on myself and others in my life. Everything I included in the boxes were vital for my journey. My valuable accomplishments, abilities, and self-worth needed to be handled with care.

I am grateful for every opportunity my former employers afforded me. Seeing how I was in a position to assist others as I loaded my boxes proved how significant achievements, awards, plaques, letters of appreciation, and other gifts are when transitioning. They not only reflect our accomplishments, but the significance of what can be done with focus, drive, and determination.

As I fully gathered my things, I was hit with this revelation: *Trust the process*.

Every lesson, experiences (good or bad) and reward are all a part of the process. As you transition, remember the trials are there to position you to triumph in your next destination. Motivational speaker, author and life coach Tony Gaskins said it best: "Trust the process, your time is coming. Just do the work and the results will handle themselves."

Before trusting the process, I knew my day of transition would come. I felt so unfulfilled in my position with the agency, I was open to a career change when the opportunity presented itself. There was more to professional life than what I had; however, I was not always clear on how to get to where I wanted to be. Once I saw the way, I took action and created a direct path towards the finish line.

If you are not sure when the time is right, pay attention – there are clues *everywhere*. How do I know? I took note of the things which came naturally, intrigued and excited me, then viewed total picture. I also gained clarity from connecting my current roles with life outside my profession. For example, I love working with people; even as a teen, I've always had compassion for others. My desire is to see others win, achieve their goals, manifest their visions, overcome obstacles and survive setbacks or disappointments. With each victory I've had, I embraced the moment and cherished each win in its own way.

Even now, my perspective has not changed personally or professionally. As I packed, I made sure to transfer items which reflected my accomplishments, skills and abilities, while exhibiting my experience as a trainer, administrator, investigator and human relations professional.

Propelling Exercises:

Based on what you've read thus far, answer this question: *What are you holding*?

Take a moment to reflect on the experiences of your career, breaking each incident into parts. Each segment should include a beginning (inciting incident or event), middle (ensuing action) and outcome (the end result/takeaway). What would you do differently the next time? Use the lines below to write your answers.

This process illuminates your previous experiences, and what should be considered to take with you along the journey. You will be pleasantly surprised how some things worked to your professional and personal advantage. Whether good or bad, that one experience could be the very thing to expose something bigger and better awaiting you.

In my case, the profession may have changed, but my focus remained the same. I wanted to be in a field where I had direct contact with people. I do not enjoy being closed in between four walls, browsing documents all day with little to no human connection.

Let's get back to you. Are you clear about what you are holding? Are the contents of your box based on professional achievements beneficial to your personal development? It would not hurt to review your entire professional history and gather everything relevant towards your change. Remember they can either serve as the foundation or the packing list to guide you through the P's: preparing, packing and positioning to propel. From this point on, create and maintain a running list of your values, credentials and experience.

Even though you know what is going in your box and may have already packed, it is not time to load the car or request an exit interview yet. There is still more work to be done before the transition.

ADD SECURITY MEASURES

When referencing security measures, I am not referring to bubble wrap or padding. I am talking education, training, and certification programs as they relate to your transition. Knowledge speaks to your credibility, attributes, personal drive, and determination that will appeal to potential employers or business connections. It's the value you bring to the table which seals the deal. This chapter is what I call *The Dealmaker*.

You may think, *Pamela, not all professions or jobs require secondary or post-graduate education*. You are right. However, what you are trying to achieve may require accredited training that awards certificates, continuing education, or certifications. Research the position, occupation, and field requirements for the areas which interest you. Regardless if it is a degree or a certification, you have achieved something for life proving you have met the requirements to perform the tasks for the career requirements.

Even as you seek training, do not negate or forget what you have previously learned. All the mandatory training classes you were forced to sit through on your previous job are great additions to your resume. You will be pleasantly surprised how that two-day, eight-hour diversity training from five years ago or the yearly forty-hour professional development class could be the very thing you need to gain a future employer's attention. Let's not forget those certificates of completion for customer service which can serve as the path to a new venture.

We often downplay training, but think about. Regardless if it is for your current position or company specific, all training includes transferrable skills. From required skills to work functions, you can apply your training to another field. It's up to you to decide what if any of it fits into your new journey. If you decide to implement it, request a copy of your training records from your employer. As time progresses, keep a detailed record of training both on and off the job.

As I prepared for my transition twelve years before retiring, I furthered my education to make myself marketable to employers. Believe me, you do not have to start as early as I did, but understanding the importance of education and the time it takes to finish provides us with enough time to complete it prior to transitioning.

I remember listening to job market gurus speaking on educational requirements for potential candidates. "Getting an undergraduate degree was not enough to stand out among the competition," one in particular said. "These days, obtaining a graduate degree is a requirement to compete in the job market."

After hearing this expressed over and over again, I eventually bought into the chatter and secured my seat in a master's degree program.

In the beginning, I chose a program that was not a clear indication of my vision for a new chapter. The degree program required several elective courses to satisfy before graduation. Through one elective, my attention shifted to the concentration of Human Resources. As time went on, I became interested in personnel development and advancement. These areas resonated with me so much, I obtained a second master's in Human Resource Management, which enabled me to meet individuals who were in the field. I learned more about the work and culture from those who were already doing the job.

While pursuing my degree, I also learned more about certification programs, which sparked curiosity about the significance the credential letters which accompanied them. For example, **PMP** stands for Project Management Professional. **SRHR** means Senior Professional in Human Resources. Individuals with these certifications are highly recognized professionals who stand out among others competing for the same job. Your field may or may not require special certification, but securing additional education supplied me with a wealth of knowledge and expanded possibilities.

In addition to furthering my education, I took on temporary assignments at work, and was exposed to new opportunities. Without complaining, I volunteered for assignments and performed additional duties. I focused on training, professional development, and position recruitment, gaining an advantage as I transitioned into my new profession as a credentialed certified International Coaching Federation (ICF) coach and consultant. It also gave me the opportunity to work as an adjunct professor for a local college.

I am glad I took advantage of various opportunities in my career, which fostered a smooth transition from one career to the next. If you believe you have not figured out the career you want to transition into, that's okay. I was not positive about mine either; however, I knew I was unfulfilled. If you are not happy with what you are doing, my question is: *What are you holding*?

Propelling Thoughts:

What are you good at that you would like to build a career in?

____

____

____

____

____

____

____

What things come easy to you professionally and personally?

____

____

____

____

____

____

____

What gives you the most excitement when you accomplish it?

____

____

____

____

____

____

How do all of these answers relate to what you are currently doing now?

____

____

____

____

____

____

____

____

____

____

As you see, the *Moving Box Methodology* requires time to examine where you are personally as opposed to professionally, as well as your abilities and feedback from others.

What are you told by others you do well?

____

____

____

____

____

____

Where do you get the most positive feedback when accomplishing a task?

____

____

____

____

____

____

How does feedback make you feel?

____

____

____

____

____

____

Compare these answers to your answers in the exercise you previously completed. Once you are clear on your specialties, it is time to explore the opportunities within the industries or positions which may be a better fit for you. This is also a great time to seek advice from those in the field you are breaking into.

To garner more skills, volunteer with different organizations connected to your interest to gain insight on the profession, and how to get started. Nothing can stop you from sealing the deal, but YOU. I must warn you though, this is the time when fear shows up, creating a domino effect of one doubt after another. The more things work and we see potential, our minds get busy and will be forced to decide how committed we are to the idea.

Let's examine the following areas: achievement, personal performance, fulfillment, and vision. Based on your thoughts, rate each one from one to ten, one being the lowest, ten the highest.

Achievement: _____

Personal Performance: _____

Fulfillment: _____

Vision: _____

Now answer these questions as it relates to these four elements:

Where do you see yourself in these areas?

____

____

____

____

____

____

____

____

Where can you improve to give yourself higher number for a chance to prepare for the next chapter?

____

____

____

____

____

____

Executing these exercises correctly provides the confidence needed to move on and get security measures in place. It also motivates us to increase our education and training, or take the entrance exam needed to qualify for the position we seek.

If you need help seeking educational opportunities, digital platforms such as LinkedIn Learning, Udemy, EdX and Skillshare offer a variety of courses in various fields. Seeking additional opportunities demonstrates constant thirst to learn, which is a great attribute in changing careers. One thing to remember is not to quit when you do not pass on your first try. Also, add additional "security" by showing decision-makers or clients how your credentials align with their mission.

Sometimes when a career change involves obtaining

degrees or training for a new certification, we tend to believe we cannot afford more debt or do not have the time to pile more on our plates. Let me encourage you – it CAN be done.

Time management was paramount in accomplishing my goals while there were so many other things competing for my attention. The various options to obtain a degree, additional training or certification are vast, especially now when many programs are being offered virtually. It is up to you; how bad do you really want this transition?

Here are some helpful tips to keep from getting overwhelmed by continuing education.

- Keep moving and do not stop until it's done.
- Stay focused on the end result.
- Make plans to accomplish your education or goal.
- Give yourself tangible deadlines, and keep important dates in front of you.
- Be realistic with your timelines.
- Rely on your strengths to accomplish your goals.
- Stay the course and see it through until it's done.
- Find an accountability partner.
- Build your endurance.

The *Moving Box Methodology* may seem overwhelming, but I have faith in you. You have to push through the process, and understand what's waiting for you on the other side. When it becomes too much, remind yourself why you got started. Ask yourself how much it means to you. Can you see the results awaiting if you complete the steps, I have shared with you? Will documenting your goals and dreams on a vision board change your perspective?

I've been creating vision boards for three years, which has been extremely instrumental in seeing my goals before I achieve them. They have been a real treat and point of gratitude when I sit down to celebrate the wins that I first documented in writing or pictures on my boards. Whether furthering your education, volunteering, or visualizing your desires by creating vision boards, when it comes to transitioning careers, it is all needed to seal the deal.

PAY ATTENTION TO LABELS

The *Moving Box Methodology* represents you and what is next. If you have done the work, both tangible and intangible items connected to who you are including experiences, abilities, and what you represent should be packed in the box.

Now that you have carefully packed and secured your box, how do you feel? Isn't this exciting? Alright, let's focus on making sure your professional voice is conveyed on your resume', vitae, application, cover letter, etc.

Your appearance on paper is the professional's first impression of you. What you document provides them with relevant information to decide if they want to learn more about, pass up or proceed with you. For many, credentials are how hiring managers or potential partners judge, so, it is imperative to understand the principles of marketing and pitching yourself.

Resumes, cover letters, applications, vitae, etc. confirms if we are a fit for an employer's company. If they are impressed, they will schedule an interview. Distributing resumes and applying for positions reflects a proactive spirit on your part, alerting employers that you are available for hire. Be careful, though - it's at this point where anxiety creeps in.

Take a deep breath, collect your thoughts, and pull yourself together. You've taken the necessary steps to develop your skills throughout your career, and there is nothing anyone could do to strip it away. Even if you are transitioning into a field that's significantly different from what you have been doing, your transferable skills can be infused in your new career. It is about making sure your qualifications are acutely conveyed, and shows the decision maker you are the best candidate for the position.

Before we move forward, let me ask: When was the last time you updated your resume and cover letter?

Allow me to share a secret with you - these two documents are a snapshot of your professional experiences, knowledge, and credentials – the key to your YES. Your resume depicts your personal background, and weighs in on whether your skills and experiences aligns with the position you are applying for. Show them you are worth investing in.

Even if your resume does not seem catchy or appear fully aligned with the company's ideal candidate, you want to give enough to spark their interest to land the interview. Personal communication has helped many people obtain opportunities that they would not have landed depending on paperwork alone.

One of the most important aspects of a resume is your career impact statement, which explains who you are, what you are about, and who cares or in other words why should the reader care. We often view this statement a summary or profile statement defining the value you bring to the company's cause, needs or wants; the important thing to remember is you as the author tailor the narrative to fit their vision.

This Side Up. Your resume provokes reader interest in you. I cannot state this enough: What's on your resume must align with their desires. Many resume writers advise clients to steer clear of including career objectives, because they are no longer critical to the resume. Be careful not to omit information pertinent to landing the position, do include details relevant to the job.

The right facts are crucial here. Even though we may not perfectly match their requirement, our resume highlights transferrable skills. What are transferrable skills? Transferrable skills are the duties we have performed in prior positions that are universal or transferable in nature. For example, if we worked in sales, the customer service skills we have acquired can transfer into healthcare.

In addition to transferrable skills, do not forget to include the soft skills – wording describing the ability to interact and work with others, which is useful in any profession. Rarely do we find careers which do not include working with others, thus making soft skills a vital highlight wherever you transition.

As I made my transition, I was not aware how many duties and responsibilities I was carrying into my next chapter until I hired a resume writer who walked me through my lengthy career. I was shocked when I saw the finished product. The skills and abilities I took for granted were actually part of the duties of several job announcements I viewed. My new resume made me ecstatic; seeing my accomplishments on paper made me swell with pride. A well-prepared resume goes a long way; however, before finding the perfect fit, my experience with resume writers was not always rewarding.

I would be remiss if I did not share my first encounter with a resume writing company. It was a complete disaster, but I was not aware at the time how bad the resume was. Previously, I was hired for jobs based on fill in the blank applications and entrance exams. After two plus decades, once I returned to the job market, resumes were key. It was apparent that I needed to have one in hand to move forward.

The first resume company I worked with produced a generalized document listing all positions I held with little descriptions and performance dates. Nothing on it was conducive to the job announcement I forwarded them, and there was no correlation between the position, my professional experience and accomplishments. I was not even asked questions to help fill in the gaps the resume writer needed.

Based on my horrific resume, I am certain the human resource staff was puzzled why I was applying for the job. I often wondered if my resume even made it through the Applicant Tracking System (ATS). If you are not familiar with ATS, take the time to research it before transitioning. Needless to say, I did not receive any responses. Once I studied and understood the process better, it was obvious why I had not received any callbacks. My resume did not speak on my behalf and failed to generate the two-way conversation needed to make an introduction. It was not a proper representation of ME and my potential to fit in to the federal jobs I was applying for. After doing my homework, I scrapped it and had a new one drafted correctly.

Before penning this book, a company offered me a position I was not qualified due to my age. Even the way I was notified of their interest was untraditional. Out of the blue, I received a private message through social media, requesting I contact a hiring manager who came across my resume and believed I was a fit for his agency. I was familiar with the position he sought to fill, and its age restriction; however, our conversation was the exact opposite of my expectations. This proves how important non-verbal communication is in pushing you to your next chapter.

Now that we understand the importance of resumes and other documents, let's incorporate the next phase of handling your box.

It is time to identify your inner critic. These are the things you tell yourself, which are the opposite of what you are trying to do. The *critic* normally says things such as: you are not good enough, you are not good at ____________________, you are not smart enough, who do you think you are, etc.

For some of us, this is a mechanism we develop to protect ourselves. It also regulates us to our comfort zone, preventing room for growth and expansion. If we allow self-criticism to take over, we will have a difficult time overcoming obstacle which could keep us stuck and from accomplishing our goals.

Let me warn you, this is the first time you will be sharing the contents of your moving box with others such as potential employers, business partners, or clients/customers. In most cases, what's presented in writing is what they will see before laying eyes on you. It is the bold writing or symbols on your box, which I call *the labels*.

Nowadays, we must keep accurate records and include inventory sheets when shipping or transferring boxed items, as accountability and handling measures for the shipper and receiver. Resumes, cover letters, applications and vitae, etc. are no different.

Even though the aforementioned documents are the first impressions strangers have of us, the more we share from our professional records, the better off we will be. If your resume does not excite you, how do you expect the decision makers to receive it?

I was super impressed when I saw how everything was captured in writing on my first well written resume'. Honestly, I never would have believed standing outside in freezing 28-degree temperatures for over twelve hours, not being able to feel my feet or hands with a runny nose during a presidential inauguration would enhance my resume, showing leadership skills, managing people and teamwork. It was a small detail that yielded big results.

Please do not recite the responsibilities from the job posting verbatim on your resume; show your worth by giving the company something to believe in. A resume is effective without being lengthy, wordy or overcompensating. Showcase your uniqueness as it compares to what they are looking for and you will hit it out the park. Employers desire tangible results and accomplishments as it relates to their future employees. Before you are awarded an interview, remember - your resume is a snapshot of you through words.

Propelling Thoughts:

Review your resume, cover letter, and any another written credentials and answer the following questions below.

What do your documents convey to the hiring manager?

____

____

____

____

____

____

Based on the job description, do your credentials prove you are the best candidate for the job? If so, what stands out to you?

____

____

____

____

____

____

If your credentials do not convey you are the best candidate, how can you strategize in order to secure the job?

____

____

____

____

____

____

You many need to conduct more research and take the time to position yourself prior to transitioning. Often, we take our "little experiences" for granted, deeming them irrelevant to our next move, when they could be the very things to propel us forward.

When I started my transition, the best thing I could have done was seek resume assistance. My first effort was a fluke, but I had time to redirect and it was corrected. There is so much help out there beneficial in preparing our *labels.* In this phase and others to come, you may realize you need help, and that's fine. A career transition differs slightly from applying for a position or seeking a promotion in a field you have extensive history in. You do not have to do this alone.

CHECK OUT THE FORWARDING ADDRESS

Now that you have decided what items to keep and those that would not serve well on your new journey, it is time to focus on your new destination.

Let's take a closer look at where you are delivering your moving box. As with any parcel, the address or shipping labels indicate the destination and method of delivery whether via mail, moving truck or carrier. In my case, I was hand-delivering my moving boxes to the next destination. I knew the address, and where I was going. As you prepare to ship your boxes, let us examine the forwarding address.

Packages are typically mailed or delivered via carrier.

To ensure they arrive at the right location to the correct person, a label is placed on the outside of the box. The postal staff reviews the mailing information to determine where the package is heading, taking into consideration the cost and estimated time of delivery.

When shipping via mail carrier, drivers use their GPS to determine the best way to make a deadline. The GPS gives clear directions, allowing room for error, redirecting the course if necessary. A few days after mailing, your box has arrived. This is an awesome invention, as I analyze it even more. This device says so much more about our journeys in anything we set out to do.

When it comes to the *Moving Box Methodology,* professional deliveries differ slightly based on our goals and dreams, which is the same for personal moves. For example, if you're looking for a new home, several factors must be considered before even thinking about buying it. Is the neighborhood safe? What are the crime statistics? Is the street busy or quiet? What is the neighborhood history?

But, there's more:

Logistically, what is the commute to and from essential locations such as work, schools, homes of family and friends or other amenities? Who are your future neighbors? Is it a single or multi-level home? Is the location a good fit for your family's lifestyle and wellbeing?

Ask yourself the same questions when selecting your future career destination. Is the company a good fit for your desires? How long is the commute to and from home? Is it located near places you frequent? What is the building makeup? Who will you be working with?

Before settling on your next destination, it is important to research and learn more about the companies you are interested in.

RESEARCH

Research requires patience.

There is no other way to put it. Impatience leads to hasty decisions. However, if you patiently conducted your research, the facts would prepare you to make the right one.

Take *Company X,* for example. Although this company has a big name, research reveals how badly they treat their employees. There are no real incentives or perks other than the big-name. In the case of *Agency Y,* research reveals although it is popular among family, friends and acquaintances, the atmosphere is toxic. Their polices are outdated and operations antiquated. There is no room for advancement, unless you play up to the decision makers. *Company Z* consistently has job openings in your desired field, with a high possibility you can secure the position. However, research reveals the company has a high turnover rate based on employee dissatisfaction for major reasons. Research breeds sound decisions. It is a matter of covering all bases before taking the leap.

The thought of extensive research can be daunting, but it must be done before shifting careers. I have heard many unfavorable stories of individuals jumping from one company to the next. Only to find out where they have landed is worse than their former position because they did not research properly. Many have found themselves moving backwards because of it. I can't express this enough: research is imperative in order to move forward.

If you are not sure how to thoroughly research a company, I can offer you tips to get it done. Most businesses provide their history, staff profiles, locations, press and legal matters, employment opportunities, and other statistical data on their websites. An internet search may reveal articles with additional details. LinkedIn and Glassdoor are great sites to visit if you want to learn more about a company, or even apply for jobs. As a matter of fact, I highly recommend reaching out to people you may know who currently work in the field or at a company for further insight.

As a coach, it would be negligent of me not to remind you to be mindful of limiting beliefs which show up during the research phase. Some information you discover can get in the way of moving forward during your transition, as favorable or unfavorable things may be uncovered as you dig deeper into the agency's background. Be cautious when reading negative stories online or listening to testimonies from family, friends or associates; even those whom you trust to provide credible intelligence.

Research is where you have to maintain an open mind and weigh your findings against your own standards. How useful is this information as it relates to your decision to move on? How will it affect you personally? Is this what you are really setting your sights on in order to move forward?

I am not advising you to ignore unfavorable information, but take it for what it is worth, keeping in mind there could be more to the version being told by the narrator or author. It is equally important to evaluate everything you come across. Workplace culture is essential in learning the history and mission of the company.

As I researched agencies, I was also in the middle of taking graduate courses. I would often speak with classmates who worked for different agencies within the federal government, which was where I originally wanted to be. For broader opportunities, I wanted to snag a job with a federal agency following my transition from local law enforcement.

I solicited my classmates to learn about their personal experiences with select agencies, since most of the ones they worked for were on my radar. Our conversations were fascinating; I saw a reoccurring pattern in many of the stories they shared with me.

The thing I noticed most was those individuals I interviewed were operating within their comfort zone. The agency was not holding them back - how they viewed themselves stunted their growth. Though enrolled in a master's program, what they believed about themselves caused them to remain stuck in their current circumstances. If you really want to understand how someone sees themselves, pay attention to how they communicate their goals, visions and dreams. It tells you everything.

For the most part, the federal retirement system is under a single umbrella. Very few of their programs deviate from the parent system, and operate from a different pay scale. Moving from one agency to another should not stop anyone from striving to advance, especially with no consequences at the end goal. In the cases of my classmates, the ultimate goal was full retirement benefits. As I listened to their stories, I carefully weighed what was useful alongside my goals, and did not allow myself to run with information without measuring it against my plans.

The next factor of research is finding out what the company wants from you. Your research should reveal what the company wants in an employee, business partner or business owner, etc. relevant to the position. Many agencies list job announcements or business opportunities, but I would advise you to scour them carefully.

If the ideal company you want to connect with does not have available openings, you can still view job descriptions on their websites (if available), or review older announcements to prepare for future opportunities.

Now please go with me for a moment. You order a beautiful green velvet dress with hints of orange and yellow (or in men's case, a hunter green suit) from an online site for the first time. You need the outfit for an event you will be attending, which has a dress code of green apparel only. You are really looking forward to attending the event, as you have always wanted to go and heard great reports about it from others.

When the package arrives on your doorstep, you do not know what to expect. Hoping the new outfit is the right fit and color so it does not have to be returned. As you carefully open the box, trying not to damage the contents, the most beautiful dress or awesome suit is revealed inside. Immediately, you hurry to try it on. It's a fantastic fit, and you are pleased. You took a chance after finding the outfit online, which turned out to be exactly what you were looking for and met all your requirements. This is how you want to present yourself to the person(s) receiving your package; the perfect fit. Doing your homework and presenting yourself in an appealing way ensures you will gain their attention - make sure your box includes everything that will get you hired.

Take time to discover what a potential employer or client wants. Balance what you bring to the table with their requirements, and when they call you for the interview, wow them with what you bring to the table. If you execute this correctly, you will be making formal greetings to the rest of the staff in no time. Unfortunately, thorough research is often overlooked, even though it can propel you past the competition.

ASK FOR HELP - HEAVY BOX

It is time to physically move your box. With all the wonderful tangibles and intangibles carefully packed inside, I cannot imagine how heavy your box is. You have sealed and protected it; it has been labeled with the destination and pertinent details. However, when you go to lift it, you cannot do it alone.

Don't you think it is time to ask for help?

My containers were overloaded with twenty-seven years' worth of my life; I had to bend my knees and lift them with my legs avoid injuring my back. I am grateful for people coming to my aid during the moving periods throughout my career. Their offers to help carry those heavy boxes was music to my ears. The extra help made moving easier, and sped up the process. Before I knew it, my valuables were in the car, and I rode off into my new journey.

Networking and asking for assistance during your move is important. This is the time to develop meaningful relationships and bridge the gap between your life's connections. Today, word of mouth is the number one tool for business success, and I do not see that changing any time soon. It is essential to make a great impression on those who can refer you later.

You would be surprised how many amazing people are looking to help others professionally, because they understand how it felt to be in your shoes and the burden of transitioning alone. On the other hand, some of them remember seamlessly transitioning into a field simply because someone helped them along the way.

Tackling your transition alone is challenging. Doing it by yourself leaves you spinning your wheels, repeating steps or quitting all together. That's why networking, socializing, and connecting with others is vital.

Far too often, we are advised to move in silence because telling others about our desire for a new career incites backlash – especially from your current boss, co-workers and others close to you. They may even handle your relationship differently once they get wind of your plans. Their interest lies with the company; filling the position once you have vacated it is their top priority, and I get it. However, their actions should not make you shut down.

There is no reason to do this by yourself - you need help. Do not be afraid to tell others what you want, but use discretion if you are concerned that sharing your plans will adversely impact your relationship with your current employer.

As you build your network, identify honorable people who are willing to share their knowledge and assist you. There are people who have no problems introducing you to game changers to help do what you are not capable of doing alone. Before requesting assistance, make sure you are serious and not wasting anyone's time. Time is a hot commodity, and something we are unable to get back. You do not want doubt to cause people to feel like you are wasting theirs.

What if I had to go back to the individuals who moved my boxes two weeks later, because I changed my mind and needed their help again? Do you think they would jump to assist a second time? Not if it appears their time is being wasted.

It is important to stand by your decision and follow through. Slacking or mismanaging people's time and efforts will be what you are remembered for. Mental images are hard to erase; how you show up or not will be the deciding factor if the person you ask is willing to help. It's a small world...negative interaction spreads like wildfire.

Have you made an effort to connect with others in the direction you are trying to go? If you believe you do not know someone already, examine your circle. What common interests do you have in reference to your goals?

American entrepreneur, author and motivational speaker Jim Rohn's quote sums up this message this way: "Show me your friends, I will show you your future."

This statement confirms how fast and if you are able to reach your goals with the people you are connected to. Consider the people in your life and identify who will hold you back, stand by without offering assistance, or help propel you forward.

I have compiled a list of people you should have in your circle during this critical time.

- Those who provide guidance, direction, support and serve as motivators.
- Those who go the distance with you on this journey.

I refer to them as your *warrior friends*. These types of friends are essential to your success. If the people in your life do not align with these indicators, keep them at bay as you pursue your dream. Quitters, complainers and naysayers are not wise counsel; they will only discourage you. They have issues with clarity, struggle with courage, lack motivation and do not have the drive to follow through on their own goals or dreams. If they are looking at their lives through tainted lenses, how can they see your vision clearly?

Like-minded people help sort things out and keep us on the right path. If you are struggling to find people who fit the criteria, do a self-check. Being unable to receive your *warrior friends* does a disservice to everyone. We must demonstrate our dedication, trustworthiness and consistency to the warriors as well. If we are not prepared for this group, they will know. We have to be prepared to seriously level up in all areas, which is not hard to do.

The decision to move on shows forward thinking. If you do not have it all figured out, go the extra mile to get prepared. Following the exercises in the essential steps builds character as well. We can connect with like-minded people who are looking for the same qualities and characteristics as we are. There is most likely someone close to us whom we may have overlooked because we had a different mindset before now.

Let me make one thing clear: the ultimate goal is

moving forward. If you do not have the types of friends in your circle I mentioned, putting your box back on the shelf is not an option. If you must, go ahead get the dolly and load up it on your own. Once you take the initiative, someone will come along to assist you. There are several platforms you can join where others are willing to answer your questions and help.

Since the early 2000's, social media has become the #1 networking tool to connect people, whether it's Facebook, Instagram, LinkedIn or Twitter. Depending on your age and influences, many shy away from joining the platforms because they do not understand the benefit social media serves, or aware of the connections to professional groups with credible business people with a wealth of knowledge, meaningful to your journey. For example, if you need certifications, social media allows users to network with those who have successfully passed the course, and can shed light on how they did it. In specialized groups, members have no problem providing assistance or pointing you in the right direction.

When used correctly, social media is also a powerful networking tool. For example, LinkedIn is a great platform to find individuals willing to help you learn about jobs, meet employers and entrepreneurs. You can also post your own credentials and communicate with contacts to learn more about companies and positions before applying.

Professional membership organizations are also good for networking. In some cases, your professional status may not be a requirement for membership to obtain information pertaining to the industry. Some organizations will allow you to join as an associate member until you officially meet their qualifications. Many share information via newsletter for upcoming conferences, people to connect with and current job listings. I have seen groups allow new members to introduce themselves during live events or in their publications, although what they share is regulated according to the group's guidelines. There are always point of contact people available to assist you and provide further information in every organization.

Despite the advancements of networking in the digital age, some of us still fear it. The whole concept of networking is often downplayed by society. How many times has someone mentioned the word networking, and you immediately think of a room crammed with people making small talk? You are in your best clothes, feeling uncomfortable as someone spouts on about themselves without letting you get a word in, then you leave with a business card and move on to the next person?

When preparing to transition, networking came to

mind for me often. In business, networking is the process of interacting with others for the purpose of developing professional and personal relationships. In order to break the fear of networking, let's identify the personality traits and how they could possibly be hindering your ability.

People are either introverts, extroverts, or ambiverts.

- An introvert prefers alone time and is selective with whom they communicate with, usually limited to their close circle. They struggle socially, and avoid it when possible.
- Extroverts are outgoing, and do not have issues speaking with others. They thrive in social environments, and welcome opportunities to speak with others.
- The ambivert is a mix between the introvert and extrovert. They enjoy alone time and socializing. Ambiverts know how to turn their social skills off and on as needed.

After years of going back and forth with this subject, I realized I am an ambivert. I often wondered how people identified as one or the other, yet their traits did not line up with the one they chose. For example, I identify as an ambivert because I love time alone, at home watching the Hallmark Channel all day on the weekend, but also prefer being around a small circle of family and friends. On the other hand, I have often found myself speaking in a room full of strangers, meeting new people from all over the world, enjoy attending a large fitness class, and finding accountability partners.

On workdays, I enjoy productive meetings, training, and reaching out to people, volunteering in the community in my spare time. After analyzing my desire for both alone time and being surrounded by people, I am truly a lover of both worlds; I know how to turn it on and off depending on the situation. Learning to deal with your personality traits is extremely helpful in transitioning if you plan to network. I recommend you take time to identify them.

Propelling Thoughts:

How do you feel about networking? What problems do you face when connecting with others?

____

____

____

____

____

____

____

Have you experienced negative networking in the past? How did it affect you?

____

____

____

____

____

____

____

What happened as a result of the situation?

____

____

____

____

____

____

Are you open to learning how to network effectively?

____

____

____

What personality trait do you best identify with?

____

____

____

____

____

____

If you identify as an introvert, allow me to offer you some advice. I completely understand networking is frightening for you, but you have to find a way to get past it in order to transition.

I suggest you revisit the list of people in your circle, and determine who falls into which trait category. If you do not have anyone to depend on during this stage, networking with others is a good way to find those who are up for the task.

If being around people is an issue for you, try inviting someone out for coffee or tea or call them on the phone. Get a calendar and schedule meetings with potential connections - this could help break you out of your shell. Even as an introvert, do not allow fear to stop you from seeking people to for help.

Communication is the key to getting the word out and get you moving in the right direction, faster. Some people would love to be in a world where they can do everything themselves without any help. However, that is not how it works. People need people in every aspect of their lives, especially in transitions. If someone says they reached their goals alone, be careful. There is always help along the way. Nobody can do this alone, so do not ever be afraid to ask for assistance.

BE PREPARED TO PROVIDE A DETAILED EXPLANATION

Is it me or does it seem whenever you are moving, someone is always curious about what's inside the boxes? When I was carrying my moving box out of the building during my transition, I was questioned about what was inside. I was not just questioned by the people helping me carry them, but from those on the sidelines watching.

What you tell hiring managers affects you securing the job. How are you describing your accomplishments, skills, and abilities? What are you saying regarding your values? This is all part of the interview process, which is your time to showcase your talents to your potential employer or client.

There is a unique twist to this process: As much as we are told to shine during the interview, you should go into it allowing your personality to breakthrough. No employer wants to hear you brag with your superhero cape on; let the interviewer meet the person they would be comfortable with being around in the workplace during business hours, as a member of their team.

Go in there knowing they want someone who is prepared to immediately meet their needs. Show them you are capable of solving their problems and getting the job done. Assure them you are the best candidate for the job, with no room for error.

Interview etiquette circles right back to doing your research. Do you align with what they are looking for? Which of your accomplishments coincides with their needs? Many people go into interviews with themselves in mind, when it should be the other way around. The interviewer has the company's mission and goals in mind; you have to convince them you are the one for the job.

This is the final presentation of your moving box. Your audience must be assured you have the know-how and potential to push the company to the next level. They may question your knowledge about the company, or you might find you share a common interest with the interviewer. They may ask about your interests, hobbies or where you're from. No matter what they ask, respond carefully. This interview is to show them you fit their need…not them fitting yours.

If interviews are not your strong suit, I recommend practicing with a friend to get more comfortable. Practice helps you learn to effectively communicate everything that makes you the best candidate for the job. If you package everything right, you will impress the interviewer. The goal is to stand; never go in trying to blend with the others. You want to walk in a candidate, and leave HIRED.

I have had the privilege of serving on several interview panels with my former agency, during mass hiring. Sitting through hours of interviews, I cannot begin to tell you how many candidates were unprepared to showcase their worth. We could tell who had done their due diligence before the interview, and who did not. Even though we had their resumes in front of us, it was up to the interviewee to sell themselves and show us the person behind the resume'.

If I had to pinpoint the most common wrong turn many applicants took, I would say there was no real connection between the person and their resumes, which is a No-No! They were not prepared to interview, and in some cases were unsure what we wanted. Out of the vast pool of candidates, there were only a few who effectively expressed their value. By the time the last interview was completed, we were scrambling for solid fits.

Some candidates did not make the cut because they failed to ineffectiveness in sharing their knowledge, skills and abilities beyond the resume. It was a great honor to serve on these panels during my tenue at the agency because not only did it help me understand the interview process, but the importance of presentation. I also discovered many things about the process I had taken for granted, which helped tremendously as time went on. Now, it helps me prepare my coaching clients for interviews and other related paths.

Children should be taught how to articulate their abilities, accomplishments and knowledge from grade school to graduation. I am not referring to an oral communication course learning various types of speeches and reciting fancy quotes. I am talking about learning how to show people your value.

Often times, we communicate mixed messages about ourselves to others. Some people say do not brag or boast about your capabilities, because people cannot stand arrogance. During your transition; however, be prepared to able to convey how the company would benefit from bringing you on board. Practice out loud. Describe all your assets to the letter, and the value they add. For example, you can say, you did X, Y, Z which led to discovering more about A, B, C - in turn saving D, E, F. Trust me - no one will slap your hand because you are talking too much. They want to hear what you have to say in order to make a sound decision.

Next, create you elevator pitch. An elevator pitch is primarily a quick, concise summary of what we can do, typically pertaining to sales. It can be implemented in the interview process as well. Elevator pitches share what's necessary, essential and required within .30 to .60 seconds. They help build confidence in expressing what we bring to the table. They also let people know we are serious about what we do. A well-crafted elevator pitch urges people to get to know us better, and opens the dialogue about how our services and skills are assets.

Think of this entire concept as its own interview. I am not saying stroll in, give a short elevator pitch and walk out the door leaving a card with your contact information. When used in interviews, the elevator pitch is best served when asked a direct question like, *"Tell me about yourself."* Remember, you are verbalizing your experience, the tools in your chest (*Moving Box*), and skills.

During this step, many of us struggle with self-worth when we are unable to articulate our value. Listening to negative self-talk pushed us away from acknowledging our worthiness and the positive things we have achieved. We shut down, rather than effective expressing ourselves to others.

Propelling Thoughts:

If this is an area of concern for you, list where you struggle most to convey your value in front of people. Consider a time when you were asked to present to a large group. How did you prepare? What was your pitch or topic? Use the lines below to answer the questions.

Who asked you to present?

____

____

How did you feel when asked?

____

____

____

____

____

____

____

____

____

What was the topic for the presentation?

____

____

____

How did you prepare?

____

____

____

____

____

____

Who was your audience?

____

____

____

____

____

____

What feedback did you receive after presentation? How did you feel once completed?

____

____

____

____

____

____

____

If you have never presented or cannot recall a moment, think about a time you had to explain to a person how to do something. Now answer the above questions, eliminating the ones which do not apply. After you have completed this exercise, you may discover something about yourself. If you recognize a pattern of negative thinking, redirect your statements into positive thoughts which exhibits confidence and positivity. This is all about self-worth. If you do not see enough in you to share with others, how will they be able to see it as well?

In this chapter, we discussed the importance of articulating the valuables inside your moving box. This is when you have to dig deep and stop at nothing to present your best self. Interviews are the bridge from where you are to where you want to be. Being nervous about it is normal. As soon as we are notified of an interview, our emotions take over.

I am going to let you in on a secret: You will survive the interview. You have everything you need, especially if you have made it this fair in the process. Your resume spoke their language, now let them hear it from your mouth. Harness your nervousness, and dial your emotions down to a manageable level. It can be done - you can do this!

The *Moving Box Essentials* help curb the anxiety transition generates. Preparation and packing builds confidence, and shifts us into a different mindset.

If you still need help with nervous energy, consider the following method I have used with my clients in preparing for oral assessments. It is called the Process of the P's, and it works.

The Process of the P's:

- ***Prepare responses based on knowledge***: You do not know what you will be asked; however, based on your research you know more than you think. Brainstorm sample questions and prepare responses accordingly.

- *Practice answering the response*: Based on what you come up with, practice your responses out loud. You can look in a mirror, audio record or rehearse with another person.
- *Pay attention*: Paying attention to your conduct, and be mindful of the interviewer's questions and instructions. Give questions careful consideration before responding. This is not the time to second-guess or doubt yourself.

If you have completed all the steps to articulate who you are to the interviewers, you are on the road to face whatever they throw at you. Remember, you are in charge of your actions; maintain control. Prior to any interview, take three deep breaths, rid yourself of coats and any loose items which can distract you, and silence your cellphone.

I landed the first job I interviewed for after being out of the job market more than two decades. I credit pre-interview research for helping me; I concentrated heavily on knowing the position I was applying for and the functions associated with it. The motivation and support I received from others in the field helped, too. As an additional measure, I joined a professional organization and read up on current trends and issues facing the industry.

I want to point out that I did not go into the interview discussing my duties as a law enforcement official. However, I answered questions the interviewers asked by connecting my transferrable skills with the position. The two hiring managers' body language told me I was on the right track.

Eventually, I relaxed and the tension in the room melted. The interviewers shook their heads and smiled in agreement, seemingly impressed by my responses. This gave me confidence I said what they wanted to hear.

After the interview concluded, I was told to step outside and someone would get back to me. Shortly afterward, they informed me that I had the position. I was shocked, but I am not sure why. After all, I prepared for the interview. Had I not been, the offer may not have been as favorable.

As the person looking to make a career transition, prepare, prepare, prepare! It takes time, as you have to pay attention to details and target what to expound on in your moving box. I suggest identifying your strengths, which can be found in what gives you fulfillment. Earlier, I mentioned one of my strengths I genuinely enjoyed was an area where I received consistent positive feedback from all sides of the coin.

Propelling Thoughts:

As you consider your transferrable skills, what comes to mind?

____

____

____

____

____

____

I want to ensure you realize how transferrable skills impact your transition. It is your job to identify what to highlight. You have everything within to accomplish your goals; anything you do not have is readily accessible. There is help at every turn, you just have to ask.

One last thought: There are no hidden tricks – the interviewer is rooting for you to be his or her next hire. They celebrate just as hard as you do when you are officially hired. The hiring manager's main objective is finding the person to fill the vacancy needed to carry out the position duties as mandated.

CONCLUSION

The best thing about the *Moving Box* is no matter where they go or what you do with them, the ultimate control is in your hands. Everyone will look to you for guidance pertaining to the box, and the articles within. If additional items are needed or something needs to be removed, you are the one deciding what goes in or comes out.

Do not be offended when people make suggestions or offer advice. There is always room for improvement; you may have to pivot if things do not work as planned. Do not give up. Remember, you are allowed to change your mind however many times you choose.

So, how did you enjoy the *Moving Box Methodology*?

Throughout this book, you have learned the essentials to be prepared, packed and propel for your transition. If you complete all of the phases and discover you are missing or may have overlooked something, you have the ability to make necessary adjustments.

For example, a new requirement has been announced by the Board of New Career Choices that was not previously in place. Now, potential candidates must complete them before hiring consideration. This is not the time to throw in the towel because you do not have everything required. That impedes your progress, and unfortunately takes away your chances for a smooth transition. Go back, unseal your box, and do whatever it takes to meet the new standards.

Knowing what and how to pack can be overwhelming and stressful. Following the essentials provides everything you need and grants you access to missing pieces. Start with yourself, then work outward. Next, look at the self(s); self-awareness, self-confidence, self-worth, and make sure you are not getting in the way of progress, then tap into outside help.

There will always be someone who has done what you are trying to do or knows someone who can help; you can seek out others on your own. You do not have to transition alone. If you have to, take a moment to breathe, work through your issues and seek additional help if needed. The essential steps are crucial in working through our emotions or negative feelings.

Let's be honest. It's hard to see what is not in front of us. When we decide to make a change, we never know what the outcome will be. I have seen end results better than I could have ever imagined, especially in being correctly aligned and prepared for the desired outcome.

You authorize what goes into, comes out of, who helps to carry and where the *Moving Box* goes. You are one hundred percent in control of its destination. There could be delays or adjustments along the way - things happen. The key is honing in on the essentials to be prepared for what lies ahead, and a chance to change course if necessary.

Enter your transition with an open mind, which allows you to change perspective as well as your habits, impressions or practices for a broader outlook. You will be able to tackle issues dealing with the self(s) mentioned earlier to prepare for the steps ahead. You will also be able to balance other perspectives as you embark on your new journey.

There is no room for a fixed mindset when you are pivoting, only to grow, learn and improve. We are continually evolving and can learn new tasks as long as we're physically and mentally capable. Your stage of life has no bearing. Preparation and packing requires you to remain open to the possibilities and have an open mind to learn and grow towards the greater cause.

As we prepare to end, I cannot stress the importance of handling your box with care. Packing takes time and effort, and it is frustrating to see one or more boxes sitting inside a garage, basement, or storage room just taking up space. Determine what is significant, gather it, pack it, and get ready to move to the next location.

The same goes with for your career transition. It serves no purpose to expend energy allowing your hard work to sit in a dark, damp, moldy space. This will not happen during your transition, especially after making the concrete decision to move towards your goals, plans and desires for your next chapter.

Remember, once you retrieve and assemble the brown cardboard paper into a sturdy moving box, keep all the essentials in mind. Your goal is to pack the necessary items - tangible and intangible, to take with you to on your way to the best version of yourself in your new role.

In summary, the essentials are as follows:

- ***Pack with caution***: Be careful when packing the *Moving Box*.
- ***Understand what you're holding:*** Know what you have, and the significance of each item for your career transition.

- ***Add security measures***: Seal and pad the box with extra security, such as additional education or training.
- ***Pay attention to labels***: What's on paper – resumes, cover letters, and applications.
- ***Check the forwarding address***: Thoroughly research potential relocations.
- ***Ask for help:*** (Heavy Box) - The importance of networking and the role people play in your transition.
- ***Be prepared to provide detailed explanations:*** Preparing for the interview.

As you prepare to move to a brighter future, you control the entire process; it can be done. You are not locked into one career, nor do you have to carry it the rest of your life. If you are no longer happy with what you are doing or if it does not serve your purpose, do something about it.

You may not know what your purpose is yet; however, you know a career transition is in order. There is more to your professional life than what you are experiencing now, but you will not know what's out there if you do not make the effort to work towards your goals, desires and dreams. I do not consider career choices mistakes – there is something to learn in every move we make.

Our last moves were full of strides and teaching moments for our next one. There is a process to everything we do. As long we take the time and do the work (include working on ourselves), we can flourish in our next endeavor. This takes true self work, which must and can be done for the greater purpose.

There is no time constraint or age limit connected to a career change; you are never too young or old. Neither is there a time limit to remain where you are. You can serve in that career for six months or forty years. The choice is yours.

If you are on the fence or hesitant to make a career transition, try working through the essentials. They are equally as important until you get ready to make a solid decision. Just know when the time comes, there will be signs which peak your future career interests.

Should you need help making your decision, I encourage you to share your interests with others and seek assistance from someone who can help you stay on course. There is help available for essential step discussed in this book. Career coaches, resume writers, job search and interview coaches can all assist with a successful career move. Professional network groups are also looking for reasons to discuss their jobs and the world revolving around them.

You do not have to make the choice alone. The world

is full of people waiting on you. A career transition is an important decision which creates a shift from the former way of doing things. Invest time into personal and professional development so you can successfully propel where you desire.

ABOUT THE AUTHOR

Pamela Burkett Jones is the executive director and founder of Proactive Life Coaching and Consulting LLC. She is a certified coach, consultant and professional speaker dedicated to supporting individuals seeking their highest potential in their professional and private lives as they move from being functional to optimal.

She is a former criminal justice professional with thirty-two years of experience: twenty-seven in law enforcement, and sixteen years in management before retiring. During her career, Pamela has created professional development and career advancement training programs. On numerous occasions, she was selected as an expert for multiple upward mobility projects. Just as she has brought her experience from one industry to the next, Pamela shows others how they can leverage their expertise and do the same.

Pamela holds a bachelor's degree in Sociology/Criminal Justice from Bowie State University and a master's degrees in Business Organization and Security Management and Human Resource Management from Webster University, as well as a criminal justice adjunct professor. In addition, Pamela hosts of a podcast titled, Taking the Lead, where she provides discussion to motivate and inspire individuals to place themselves first on their priority list.

When she is not helping clients, instructing her students, training, speaking or hosting her podcast, she enjoys participating in outdoor exercises such as biking, running, or walking year-round. She is married to her husband Preston "Lamar" and has two sons, Justin and Jalen.

To learn more about Pamela, her coaching, products, and other services, visit: www.liveproactively.com.

ACKNOWLEDGEMENTS

I am grateful for my family who continues to support and encourage me along the way allowing me to see, plan and conquer my goals and aspirations.

Very special thanks to my husband, Preston "Lamar" of twenty-six years who gives me the much-needed space to be my nature self as I follow my life long personal and professional vision and goals. His strong support during all of my endeavors as I seek to maximize my potential has been absolutely amazing.

Thanks to my intelligent sons, Justin and Jalen for always willing to assist me in any way possible in the form of a running errands, preparing meals, providing coffee or any other gestures to provide a comfortable environment as I remained dedicated to writing this book.

I want to acknowledge my tech savvy web designer sister, Zaneta Burkett Thurston for creating and managing my website where I am able to offer my products and services which were designed to help others to live a proactive life full of possibilities chasing their dreams to conquer one goal after another.

Lastly, thank you to everyone who has help me on my journey providing support, a gentle push and especially believed in me.

CPSIA information can be obtained
at www.ICGtesting.com
Printed in the USA
BVHW041254060321
601906BV00020B/810